MIMI and JEAN-PAUL'S CAJUN MARDI GRAS

MIMI *and* JEAN-PAUL'S CAJUN MARDI GRAS

**Elizabeth Moore
and Alice Couvillon**

**Illustrated by
Marilyn Carter Rougelot**

PELICAN PUBLISHING COMPANY
Gretna 1996

*Elizabeth Moore dedicates this book
to her mother, Miriam Leguenec Butler, who grew
up in the Cajun town of Abbeville; and to her grandchildren,
Elizabeth, Isabelle, R. J., and Anneliese.*

*Alice Couvillon dedicates this book
to her parents, Peter and Gloria Wilbert,
and to her Cajun husband, Robert.*

Library of Congress Cataloging-in-Publication Data

Moore, Elizabeth.
    Mimi and Jean-Paul's Cajun Mardi Gras / Elizabeth Moore and Alice
Couvillon ; illustrated by Marilyn Carter Rougelot.
        p. cm.
    Summary: Mimi visits her cousin Jean-Paul during the celebration
of Cajun Mardi Gras in Louisiana.
    ISBN 1-56554-069-7 (hardcover)
    [1. Mardi Gras—Fiction. 2. Louisiana—Fiction. 3. Cajuns-
-Fiction.] I. Couvillon, Alice. II. Rougelot, Marilyn Carter,
ill. III. Title.
PZ7.M78325Mi 1996
[E]—dc20   95-31612
                                                          CIP
                                                           AC

Manufactured in Hong Kong

Published by Pelican Publishing Company, Inc.
1101 Monroe Street, Gretna, Louisiana 70053

MIMI AND JEAN-PAUL'S
CAJUN MARDI GRAS

Jean-Paul swung on the creaky, old gate. He liked to hear the hinges groan and squeak as he went faster and faster. He dragged his toes in the warm dust until big clouds rolled up to the top of his jeans.

"Ti-Jean," his mother cried out as she opened the screen door, "What is all of that noise? And look at your jeans, they have turned brown!"

"Maman, I'm waiting for Mimi and Papa to come from New Orleans. They should be here soon."

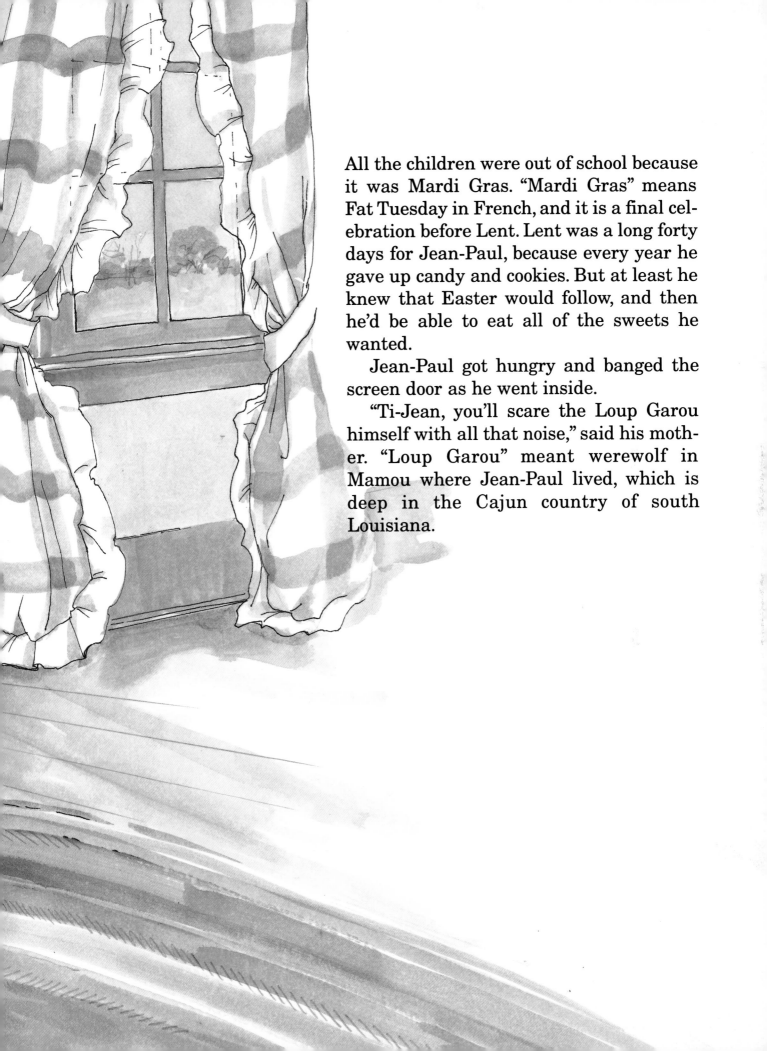

All the children were out of school because it was Mardi Gras. "Mardi Gras" means Fat Tuesday in French, and it is a final celebration before Lent. Lent was a long forty days for Jean-Paul, because every year he gave up candy and cookies. But at least he knew that Easter would follow, and then he'd be able to eat all of the sweets he wanted.

Jean-Paul got hungry and banged the screen door as he went inside.

"Ti-Jean, you'll scare the Loup Garou himself with all that noise," said his mother. "Loup Garou" meant werewolf in Mamou where Jean-Paul lived, which is deep in the Cajun country of south Louisiana.

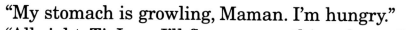

"My stomach is growling, Maman. I'm hungry."

"All right, Ti-Jean, I'll fix you something that will stop that."

Maman got out a crusty loaf of French bread that was still warm from the oven. Then she cut off the end slice. "You get the best piece, Ti-Jean. I'll give you *le nez*." *Nez* meant nose, and the end of the bread did look like a long nose. Maman pulled out some of the soft dough and spread the inside of the cone with sweet cream butter. She took some thick *la cuite*, or sugarcane syrup, and filled up the bread like a cup.

"Mmmmm, that's good. That will hold me until Mimi gets here," said Jean-Paul.

Jean-Paul went outside and called Bourré, his Catahoula hound dog. "Bourré, I wish that Mimi would get here fast, fast!"

Just as he said that, Jean-Paul spotted puffs of dust down the road and ran to see what it was. Soon he could make out his father's bright blue pickup truck and saw Mimi sitting in the front seat. The truck squealed to a stop in front of the house, and Mimi jumped out.

"*Allo*, Mimi, *comment ça va?*" asked Jean-Paul.

"Hello, Jean-Paul! You know I don't speak French—what did you say?"

"That's the way we say, 'How are you?' We speak both French and English here in Mamou."

"I'm so glad to be here, Jean-Paul. I can't wait for the Cajun Mardi Gras! You and Uncle Rabbit will have to tell me all about it." Uncle Rabbit's name was really Robert, but everyone in Mamou had called him Rabbit from the time he was a little boy.

Mimi's aunt came running out of the house and gave Mimi a big hug and a kiss.

"*Chère*, you are a beautiful sight to see!" she said. "How are your mama and daddy?"

Mimi told her aunt, whom she called Tante Conette, all of the family news as they walked into the cozy house that smelled of the spicy jambalaya simmering in the kitchen.

After they had eaten, they brought their pecan pie dessert outside and sat on the porch. The stars were bright, and the moon spilled silver light over the rice fields in the distance.

"All right, Uncle Rabbit, I know about the Mardi Gras in New Orleans," said Mimi. "Please tell me about the Cajun Mardi Gras."

Uncle Rabbit tapped the sweet-smelling perique tobacco in his pipe and took a long time to light it. Mimi wished that he'd hurry up, and she squirmed impatiently.

"Mimi, our Mardi Gras goes back further in time than your New Orleans Mardi Gras. Hundreds of years ago, in a place called France, the poor farmers did not have much to eat in the winter. When all of the food was gone, the rich people let them beg from house to house. As years passed, the begging day turned into a holiday. The farmers would mock the kings, queens, bishops, and teachers by dressing like them, but in rags and tatters. When the French Acadians, or Cajuns, settled in Louisiana more than two hundred years ago, they brought this old custom with them."

"Do you say, 'Throw me something, mister,' and catch beads and doubloons off of the floats?" asked Mimi.

"It's totally different, you'll see. But, I guarantee that you'll have a good time," said Uncle Rabbit as he got up and stretched. "It's been a long day—it's time for us to go to bed."

The sun was shining when Mimi woke up and quickly dressed. When she walked into the kitchen, Jean-Paul was already eating his *coush-coush*, or fried cornmeal topped with steaming hot milk. Tante Conette poured a huge cup of *café au lait* for Mimi. Mimi stirred in two spoons of condensed milk and sipped the delicious milk-coffee.

After breakfast, Tante Conette pulled out a mask shaped like a face but made out of window screen and said, "We'll get your costumes together, but first let's finish Papa's mask."

"I've never seen a screen mask!" said Mimi.

"*Chère*, you cannot see who is behind them, they are cool, and they are easy to see through," said Tante Conette. Mimi and Jean-Paul watched as she painted two big eyes, a zigzag mouth, and round, red cheeks. "Now we'll know which masker is Papa on Tuesday during the *Courir du Mardi Gras*. That's what we say here, Mimi,—it means 'running Mardi Gras.'"

"Guess what, Mimi—we have a surprise for you!" said Jean-Paul. "Can we show her now, Maman?"

"*Mais oui*, Ti-Jean, run and get it."

"A surprise? What is it?" asked Mimi.

In a few minutes, Jean-Paul raced back into the room wearing his costume and holding an identical one for Mimi.

"Maman and I made this costume for you, Mimi. We're both going to be clowns."

Mimi put the tall, pointed hat on her head and slipped on the fringed shirt. "I do feel like a clown, but I've never seen a clown like this!"

"In Mamou, we call a clown a *paillasse*," explained Tante Conette. "Years ago, we'd stuff straw in the sleeves."

"It must have been itchy," laughed Mimi.

Early Mardi Gras morning, Tante Conette peeked in the bedroom and whispered to the children, "*Allons!* Let's go! We don't want to miss the riders."

Mimi and Jean-Paul jumped out of bed and dressed in their costumes.

"Where's Uncle Rabbit?" asked Mimi.

"He saddled the horse and went into town at dawn to be ready for running Mardi Gras," answered Tante Conette. "They'll soon be coming down the road. Hop in the truck and we'll go meet them."

They arrived at their neighbor's house and joined friends waiting on the porch. Soon Mimi heard the sound of horses' hooves in the distance.

"Come see! Come see!" screamed Jean-Paul. "Here come the Mardi Gras!"

They all watched as the masked riders came closer. A man dressed in a purple, gold, and green cape raised a white flag. "It's Le Capitaine, the captain," said Jean-Paul. "He's in command."

Mimi listened as Le Capitaine asked permission for the riders to approach. When the neighbor nodded yes, Le Capitaine dipped his flag, and the riders charged the house.

Mimi wondered what was going on, then she heard music. The band members who sat in the truck cart played an accordion, a fiddle, and a triangle, which was called a ting-a-ling. They played "La Chanson de Mardi Gras," the Mardi Gras song and other songs that Tante Conette called "chank-a-chank" tunes.

When the riders dismounted, they danced and sang as the people on the porch cheered. One masked man lifted up Mimi and whirled her around the yard. She was frightened until she recognized the mask her aunt had designed and realized it was Uncle Rabbit.

Mimi was amazed to see the neighbor walk to the front of the house with a live, squawking chicken. She watched as he tossed it through the air into the middle of the circle of maskers. The men scrambled around the yard chasing the chicken. One man dove to the ground and grabbed the flapping chicken by its legs and held it up to the crowd to see. They clapped as he handed it to Le Capitaine, who placed it in a cage.

Mimi nudged Jean-Paul. "What's the chicken for?"

"It's for the big gumbo tonight in town," said Jean-Paul. "They'll get more chickens, onions, rice, and peppers at other houses."

Mimi was wide-eyed when she heard Le Capitaine blow a cowhorn as the maskers mounted their horses and rode on.

Tante Conette said, "Let's go to town—it won't be long before the men finish running Mardi Gras, and they'll be hungry."

Crowds lined the main street to applaud the Mardi Gras as they rode through town. Jean-Paul shouted out:

**"Mardi Gras! Chique a la paille
Run, run, run! Ti Yiiii Yiiiii!
Give me your nose,
And I'll bake you a pie."**

Some of the riders held out their hands to the crowd and begged for coins saying, *"Cinq sous! Cinq sous!"* and people dug into their pockets for change. The Mardi Gras song was played over and over, and everyone danced. Big pots of chicken gumbo bubbled on the burners and filled the air with a delicious scent.

Uncle Rabbit joined his family. "*Allo*, Mimi," he said. "Was this like your Mardi Gras in New Orleans?"

"It's really different, but lots of fun."

Uncle Rabbit took off his screen mask and handed it to Mimi. "Here, Mimi, you take this back to the city and tell all of your friends about the Cajun Mardi Gras. There's nothing like it anywhere in the world, and it is important that we keep these old traditions alive."

"*Merci beaucoup, Monsieur*," said Mimi.

"*Très bon, chère*," said Uncle Rabbit. "You'll make a fine little Cajun."